Title:
Achieving Financial Stability: An AI-Powered Guide to Using Financial Tools

by-Aviral Anand Mishra

Table of Contents:

- Retirement Savings Plans
- Types of Retirement Accounts
- Retirement Planning Strategies
- Retirement Income Sources

Chapter 6: Insurance and Risk Management

- Types of Insurance
- Choosing the Right Insurance Coverage
- Risk Management Strategies
- Insurance and Estate Planning

Chapter 7: Tax Planning

- Understanding the Tax System
- Tax Planning Strategies
- Tax Deductions and Credits
- Tax-Advantaged Investment Options

Chapter 8: Estate Planning

- Importance of Estate Planning
- Types of Wills and Trusts
- Choosing Executors and Trustees
- Estate Planning for Business Owners

Chapter 9: Financial Tools for Business Owners

- Financial Management for Small Business Owners

ABOUT ALL CHAPTERS

Chapter 1: Introduction to Financial Stability

This chapter lays out the foundation for the book, defining financial stability, and discussing why it is essential. Financial stability refers to the ability to maintain a comfortable standard of living while effectively managing financial resources. The chapter also discusses factors that impact financial stability, such as unexpected expenses, debt, and the economy's performance.

Chapter 2: Understanding Your Finances

This chapter delves into the importance of understanding one's finances, including creating a budget, tracking expenses, identifying income sources, and managing debt. Budgeting is the cornerstone of financial management, as it allows individuals to make informed decisions about spending, saving, and investing. The chapter also explores different methods for tracking expenses and managing debt, including the snowball and avalanche methods.

Chapter 3: Savings and Investment Strategies

This chapter discusses the different types of savings accounts and investments available and provides guidance on creating a diversified investment portfolio. It also covers investment strategies for different life stages, such as early career, mid-career, and retirement. Additionally, it highlights the importance of investing in assets that align with personal goals, risk tolerance, and time horizon.

Chapter 4: Credit and Debt Management

This chapter examines types of credit, managing credit card debt, managing student loan debt, and understanding credit scores. It is essential to understand how credit works, how to manage it responsibly, and how it affects credit scores. The chapter also discusses the long-term impacts of debt and provides tips for paying off debt, such as creating a debt repayment plan.

Chapter 5: Retirement Planning

This chapter covers the different retirement savings plans available, such as 401(k) plans and IRAs, as well as strategies for retirement planning, including calculating retirement expenses and selecting retirement income sources. Additionally, it discusses the importance of starting retirement planning early and highlights common mistakes to avoid when planning for retirement.

Chapter 6: Insurance and Risk Management

This chapter explores the different types of insurance, including life insurance, long-term care insurance, and disability insurance. It also provides guidance on choosing the right insurance coverage, managing risk, and incorporating insurance into estate planning.

Chapter 7: Tax Planning

This chapter covers the basics of the tax system, tax planning strategies, tax deductions, and credits. It also provides guidance *on tax-advantaged investment options, such as 529 plans and Health Savings Accounts (HSAs).*

Chapter 8: Estate Planning

This chapter delves into estate planning, including the different types of wills and trusts available, choosing executors and trustees, and estate planning for business owners. It highlights the importance of estate planning and provides guidance on incorporating estate planning into a comprehensive financial plan.

Chapter 9: Financial Tools for Business Owners

This chapter covers financial management for small business owners, accounting software, business loans and financing options, and business insurance. It provides guidance on selecting the right financial tools and strategies for achieving financial stability and long-term success.

Chapter 10: Financial Planning for Life Events

This chapter explores financial planning for significant life events, including marriage and family, divorce, career changes, and health issues. It highlights the importance of adjusting financial plans to reflect changing life circumstances and provides guidance on common financial issues that arise during these events.

Chapter 11: Conclusion

This chapter summarizes the book's key themes, including the benefits of financial stability, long-term financial planning, and taking action to achieve financial stability. It encourages readers to take the knowledge they have gained and put it into practice in their own lives.

In conclusion, this book provides a comprehensive guide to achieving financial stability, covering a range of financial topics, including budgeting, investing, retirement planning, insurance, tax planning, and estate planning. Each chapter provides practical guidance and tools that readers can use to improve their financial situation and achieve.

Chapter 1: Introduction to Financial Stability

"The best way to predict your future is to create it." - Abraham Lincoln

Financial stability refers to the ability to effectively manage financial resources and maintain a comfortable standard of living. This chapter provides an introduction to financial stability, its importance, factors that impact it, and the benefits of achieving it.

1: Understanding Financial Stability

This sub-category delves into the concept of financial stability and why it is crucial. Financial stability means being able to meet current and future financial obligations while having enough money to pay for emergencies, unexpected expenses, and achieve personal financial goals. Achieving financial stability provides a sense of security, which leads to a better quality of life, less stress, and improved mental and physical health. It also provides individuals with the freedom to pursue personal goals and passions, such as starting a business, traveling, or saving for retirement.

2: Factors That Impact Financial Stability

The factors that can impact financial stability, including economic conditions, employment status, income, expenses, and debt. Economic conditions play a significant role in financial stability as economic downturns can lead to job loss, decreased income, and increased expenses, making it difficult for individuals to maintain financial stability.

Employment status and income also play a vital role in financial stability, as stable employment and a consistent income provide the financial security needed to achieve long-term financial goals. Managing expenses and creating a budget is crucial for achieving financial stability, as it is essential to identify necessary expenses and prioritize these expenses over discretionary spending. Debt is another factor that can impact financial stability, and managing debt and creating a plan to pay it off is crucial for achieving financial stability.

3: Benefits of Financial Stability

The benefits of achieving financial stability. Achieving financial stability provides many benefits, including improved mental and physical health, reduced financial stress, and increased opportunities for personal and professional growth. Financial stability provides a sense of security, which allows individuals to take more significant risks, such as starting a business or investing in a new venture. Additionally, it provides the financial freedom needed to pursue personal goals, such as travel or hobbies.

Conclusion:

In conclusion, understanding financial stability is crucial for achieving long-term financial security. This chapter provides an introduction to financial stability, including its definition, factors that impact it, and the benefits of achieving it. To achieve financial stability, it is essential to create a financial plan that considers economic conditions, employment status, income, expenses, and debt. By doing so, individuals can enjoy the benefits of financial stability, including improved mental and physical health, reduced financial stress, and increased opportunities for personal and professional growth.

"Don't wait for opportunity, create it." - George Bernard Shaw

Chapter 2: Budgeting Techniques

"A budget tells us what we can't afford, but it doesn't keep us from buying it." - William Feather

1: The Importance of Budgeting

Budgeting is a fundamental tool for achieving financial stability. Budgeting allows individuals to identify necessary expenses, prioritize spending, and avoid overspending. It also helps individuals identify areas where they can reduce expenses, allowing them to save more money and achieve their financial goals faster.

2: Creating a Budget

This covers the process of creating a budget, including identifying income, expenses, and financial goals. Creating a budget involves understanding how much money is coming in, how much is going out, and where it is going. By understanding these factors, individuals can create a budget that is realistic and achievable.

Creating a budget involves several steps to determine your income, expenses, and allocate your income to cover your expenses. First, identify all sources of income to figure out how much money you bring in each month. Then, list all of your expenses, including fixed expenses such as rent/mortgage, car payments, and insurance, as well as variable expenses like groceries, dining out, and entertainment.

It's important to prioritize your expenses in order of necessity, such as housing, food, and transportation. Allocate your income to cover your top priority expenses first, and then distribute the remaining funds to cover your other expenses. To track your spending and monitor your progress, use a spreadsheet or budgeting app to keep track of your spending.

Using your budget effectively involves several steps. The first and most important step is to stick to your budget and avoid overspending. It may require you to make some sacrifices, such as cutting back on dining out or entertainment expenses.

Review your budget on a regular basis to ensure that you are staying on track. This may involve making adjustments to your budget as necessary to account for unexpected expenses or changes in income. Using cash instead of credit can help you stay within your budget by limiting your spending to the cash you have on hand.

It's essential to set aside some money each month for emergencies, such as car repairs or medical expenses. This can help you avoid dipping into other parts of your budget to cover unexpected expenses.

By creating a budget and using it effectively, you can take control of your finances and work towards achieving your financial goals.

3: Budgeting Techniques

This covers different budgeting techniques, including the envelope method, the 50/30/20 rule, and zero-based budgeting. These techniques can help individuals manage their finances more effectively and achieve their financial goals faster.

The 50/30/20 rule is a budgeting technique that involves dividing your after-tax income into three categories: needs, wants, and savings. The rule suggests allocating 50% of your income towards essential expenses, 30% towards discretionary spending, and 20% towards savings and debt repayment.

To use the 50/30/20 rule, follow these steps:

- Determine your after-tax income. This is the amount of money you have left over after taxes and other deductions are taken out of your paycheck.

- Divide your income into the three categories: needs, wants, and savings. Allocate 50% of your income towards essential expenses like housing, transportation, groceries, utilities, and healthcare. Allocate 30% towards discretionary spending, such as dining out, entertainment, vacations, and hobbies. Finally, allocate the remaining 20% towards savings and debt repayment.

- Track your spending to ensure you are staying within your budget. Use a spreadsheet, budgeting app, or other tools to monitor your expenses.

- Adjust your budget as necessary to account for changes in income or unexpected expenses. Make sure to prioritize savings and debt repayment, and avoid overspending in the discretionary spending category.

Here's an example of how the 50/30/20 rule might work in practice:

Let's say your after-tax income is $4,000 per month. Using the 50/30/20 rule, you would allocate your income as follows:

Needs: $2,000 (50%) for essential expenses like rent/mortgage, utilities, transportation, and groceries.

Wants: $1,200 (30%) for discretionary spending like dining out, entertainment, and vacations.

Savings: $800 (20%) for savings and debt repayment like building an emergency fund, paying down debt, or contributing to a retirement account.

By using the 50/30/20 rule, you can ensure that you are meeting your essential needs, while also allowing yourself some flexibility to enjoy discretionary spending, and prioritize savings and debt repayment. This budgeting technique can help you achieve financial stability and work towards achieving your financial goals.

Envelope system: The envelope system involves creating a separate envelope for each spending category and allocating a certain amount of cash to each envelope at the start of the month. Once the cash in the envelope runs out, you cannot spend any more in that category for the month. To use this technique, follow these steps:

- Identify your spending categories and create a separate envelope for each one.

- Determine your budget for each category and put that amount of cash in the corresponding envelope.

- Only use the cash in the envelopes for each category, and stop spending once the cash in the envelope runs out.

Example: Let's say you have envelopes for categories such as groceries, dining out, entertainment, and transportation. You allocate $200 for groceries, $100 for dining out, $50 for entertainment, and $100 for transportation. Once the cash in each envelope is spent, you cannot spend any more in that category for the month.

Zero-based budget: The zero-based budget involves assigning every dollar of income a specific purpose, so that your income minus your expenses equals zero. To use this technique, follow these steps:

- Determine your total income for the month.

- Create a list of all your expenses for the month, including fixed expenses like rent/mortgage and variable expenses like groceries and entertainment.

- Assign each dollar of income to a specific expense, so that your income minus your expenses equals zero.

Example: Let's say your income for the month is $4,000, and your expenses include rent ($1,000), groceries ($500), entertainment ($200), and debt repayment ($500). You would allocate $2,800 towards those expenses and allocate the remaining $1,200 towards savings, investments, or other financial goals.

80/20 rule: The 80/20 rule involves allocating 80% of your income towards expenses and 20% towards savings and investments. To use this technique, follow these steps:

- Determine your after-tax income.

- Allocate 80% of your income towards expenses like rent/mortgage, utilities, groceries, and entertainment.

- Allocate the remaining 20% towards savings and investments.

Example: Let's say your after-tax income is $5,000 per month. Using the 80/20 rule, you would allocate $4,000 towards expenses and $1,000 towards savings and investments.

Pay yourself first: This technique involves prioritizing savings by setting aside a portion of your income towards savings and investments before paying for other expenses. To use this technique, follow these steps:

- Determine the amount you want to save each month.

- Set up an automatic transfer from your checking account to your savings account for that amount.

- Pay for other expenses with the remaining income.

Example: Let's say you want to save $500 per month. You would set up an automatic transfer for $500 from your checking account to your savings account at the beginning of the month. Then you would use the remaining income to pay for your expenses. This technique helps ensure that you prioritize savings and investments, and avoid overspending.

A 401(k) plan is a retirement savings plan offered by an employer to its employees. The plan allows employees to contribute a portion of their pre-tax income into the account, which can then be invested in a range of options such as mutual funds, stocks, and bonds. The contributions made by employees into their 401(k) accounts are not taxed until they withdraw the money during their retirement. The plan has several benefits, including the ability to save for retirement with pre-tax dollars, the potential for tax-deferred growth, and the ability to take advantage of employer matching contributions.

To use a 401(k) plan effectively, it is essential to understand the rules and regulations associated with the plan. Some of the key things to keep in mind when using a 401(k) plan include:

1. Contribution Limits: The contribution limit for 401(k) plans is $19,500 per year for individuals under age 50 and $26,000 for those over age 50. It is essential to make sure that you are contributing enough to take full advantage of any employer matching contributions.
2. Investment Options: Most 401(k) plans offer a range of investment options, including mutual funds, stocks, and bonds. It is important to diversify your investments to reduce risk and ensure that you have a well-balanced portfolio.
3. Vesting: Vesting refers to the amount of time you need to work for an employer before you are entitled to the employer's matching contributions. Understanding your vesting schedule can help you make informed decisions about your contributions and ensure that you are taking full advantage of your employer's benefits.
4. Withdrawal Penalties: Withdrawals from a 401(k) account before the age of 59 ½ are subject to a 10% penalty, in addition to taxes. It is essential to keep this in mind when making decisions about withdrawing money from your account.

Example:
Samantha is a 35-year-old accountant who works for a large firm. Her employer offers a 401(k) plan, and Samantha has decided to start contributing to the plan. She decides to contribute 10% of her salary, which is $60,000 per year. Her employer also offers a 50% match on the first 6% of her contributions. This means that Samantha's employer will contribute an additional $1,800 to her account each year.

Samantha decides to invest her contributions in a mix of mutual funds and stocks to diversify her portfolio. She also regularly reviews her investments and adjusts her allocation based on her retirement goals and risk tolerance.

As Samantha approaches retirement age, she begins to shift her investments towards more conservative options to protect her savings. She also starts to consider when she will begin taking withdrawals from her account, taking into account the potential tax implications of her decisions. By using a 401(k) plan effectively, Samantha is able to save for retirement while also taking advantage of her employer's contributions and minimizing her tax liability.

Chapter 3: Savings and Investment Strategies

"Don't tell me what you value, show me your budget, and I'll tell you what you value." - Joe Biden

Saving and investing are important aspects of achieving financial stability. This chapter provides an overview of the different savings and investment strategies that can help you grow your wealth over time.

1. **Types of Savings Accounts:** There are different types of savings accounts available, each with its own benefits and drawbacks.

    Some of the most common types of savings accounts include:

- Basic Savings Account: This is a simple savings account that usually offers a low interest rate but has no minimum balance requirement.
- Money Market Account: This type of savings account offers a higher interest rate than a basic savings account but may require a higher minimum balance.
- Certificate of Deposit (CD): A CD is a type of savings account that offers a fixed interest rate for a specified term, such as six months or one year. Early withdrawal penalties may apply.
- High-Yield Savings Account: This type of savings account offers a higher interest rate than a basic savings account but may require a higher minimum balance or limit the number of withdrawals per month.

2. **Types of Investments:** There are different types of investments that you can use to grow your wealth over time.

    Some of the most common types of investments include:

- Stocks: Stocks represent ownership in a company and offer the potential for high returns but also come with high risk.

- Bonds: Bonds are a type of debt security that offer a fixed rate of return but usually have lower returns than stocks.
- Mutual Funds: Mutual funds pool money from multiple investors to invest in a diversified portfolio of stocks, bonds, and other securities.
- Exchange-Traded Funds (ETFs): ETFs are similar to mutual funds but trade like stocks on an exchange.

3. **Creating a Diversified Investment Portfolio:**
   Diversification is important to reduce risk and improve returns. You can achieve diversification by investing in different asset classes, such as stocks, bonds, and cash, and within those asset classes by investing in different companies or sectors. For example, instead of investing all your money in one stock, you can invest in a mutual fund that holds a diversified portfolio of stocks.

Creating a diversified investment portfolio is an essential part of achieving financial stability. Here are a few techniques for diversifying your investments:

- **Asset Allocation:**
   Asset allocation is the process of dividing your investments among different asset classes, such as stocks, bonds, and cash. The idea behind asset allocation is to balance risk and reward by investing in a mix of assets that have different levels of risk and return. For example, if you are young and have a long investment horizon, you may allocate a larger percentage of your portfolio to stocks, which tend to

have higher potential returns but also higher risk. On the other hand, if you are close to retirement, you may allocate a larger percentage of your portfolio to bonds, which tend to be less risky but also have lower potential returns.

- **Investment in Mutual Funds:**

    Mutual funds are an excellent way to diversify your investment portfolio without having to invest in individual stocks or bonds. Mutual funds pool money from multiple investors to purchase a diversified mix of securities. By investing in mutual funds, you can access a diversified portfolio of stocks or bonds that have been selected by professional fund managers.

- **Investing in Exchange-Traded Funds (ETFs):**

    ETFs are similar to mutual funds, but they are traded on stock exchanges like individual stocks. ETFs offer low fees and can provide investors with exposure to different asset classes, such as stocks, bonds, and commodities. For example, an investor could buy an ETF that tracks the performance of the S&P 500 index, which represents the performance of the 500 largest publicly traded companies in the US.

- **Investing in Real Estate:**

    Investing in real estate can be a good way to diversify your portfolio. Real estate investments can provide a steady stream of rental income and can also appreciate in value over time. An investor can invest in real estate directly by purchasing a rental property, or they can invest indirectly by purchasing shares in a real estate investment trust (REIT).

- **Investing in International Markets:**

  Investing in international markets can provide diversification benefits by exposing investors to different economic and political conditions. International investments can be made through mutual funds, ETFs, or by purchasing individual stocks or bonds.
  In conclusion, creating a diversified investment portfolio is crucial to achieving financial stability. By using techniques like asset allocation, investing in mutual funds, ETFs, real estate, and international markets, investors can reduce their risk and potentially increase their returns. It is essential to keep in mind that diversification does not guarantee a profit or protect against losses, but it can help manage risk over the long term.

4. Investment Strategies for Different Life Stages:

Your investment strategy may vary depending on your life stage and financial goals. For example:

- Early Career: When you are early in your career, you may have a higher risk tolerance and can afford to invest more aggressively in stocks.
- Mid-Career: As you approach middle age, you may want to shift your investments to more conservative options, such as bonds, to reduce risk.
- Pre-Retirement: As you near retirement, you may want to focus on income-generating investments, such as dividend-paying stocks or bonds.
- Retirement: During retirement, you may want to focus on capital preservation and income generation, such as by investing in annuities or bonds.
-

By using a combination of these savings and investment strategies, you can build wealth over time and achieve financial stability. However, it's important to remember that investing always involves some degree of risk, and it's important to consult with a financial advisor before making any major investment decisions.

Investment strategies can differ depending on a person's life stage, risk tolerance, and financial goals.

Here are **five investment strategies that are appropriate for different life stages**:
1. Dollar-Cost Averaging: This strategy involves investing a fixed amount of money at regular intervals, regardless of the current price of the investment. This approach helps to average out the price of the investment over time, reducing

the impact of market fluctuations. For example, a young person who has just started their first job could use dollar-cost averaging to invest a fixed amount of money into a retirement account, such as a 401(k), each paycheck.

2. Value Investing: Value investing involves identifying undervalued assets that have strong fundamentals, such as a low price-to-earnings ratio or high dividend yield. This strategy can be appropriate for mid-career individuals who have a longer time horizon for their investments. For example, a person in their 40s might consider investing in stocks or mutual funds that have a history of consistent dividend payments.

3. Growth Investing: Growth investing involves investing in companies that are expected to experience rapid growth in the future. This strategy can be appropriate for younger individuals with a long time horizon who are willing to take on more risk. For example, a person in their 20s might consider investing in technology companies that have a high potential for growth.

4. Asset Allocation: Asset allocation involves diversifying investments across different asset classes, such as stocks, bonds, and real estate, in order to reduce risk. This strategy can be appropriate for individuals who are approaching retirement age and are looking to reduce risk in their portfolio. For example, a person in their 50s might consider shifting some of their investments from stocks to bonds to reduce risk.

5. Tax-Loss Harvesting: Tax-loss harvesting involves selling investments that have decreased in value in order to offset gains from other investments and reduce taxes owed. This strategy can be appropriate for individuals of all ages who have taxable investment accounts. For example, a person might sell a stock that has decreased in value and use the loss to offset capital gains taxes owed on other investments.

In summary, investment strategies can differ based on a person's life stage and financial goals. By using appropriate investment strategies, individuals can create a diversified investment portfolio that meets their financial needs and helps them achieve their long-term goals.

"The stock market is a device for transferring money from the impatient to the patient." - Warren Buffett

Chapter 4: Credit and Debt Management

"Too many people spend money they haven't earned, to buy things they don't want, to impress people they don't like." - Will Rogers

Credit and debt management is a crucial aspect of financial stability. In this chapter, we will explore different types of credit, how to manage credit card and student loan debt, and how to understand credit scores.

Types of Credit:
1. Credit Cards - Credit cards are a type of revolving credit, which means you can borrow money up to a certain limit, and you pay interest on the balance you carry.
2. Personal Loans - Personal loans are typically installment loans that allow you to borrow a fixed amount of money and pay it back over a set period with interest.
3. Mortgages - Mortgages are secured loans used to buy a house or other property. The property itself serves as collateral for the loan.
4. Auto Loans - Auto loans are used to finance the purchase of a car. Like mortgages, they are secured loans, and the car itself serves as collateral.

5. Lines of Credit - Lines of credit are similar to credit cards, except they typically have lower interest rates and higher credit limits.

Managing Credit Card Debt:

1. Pay More Than the Minimum - Paying more than the minimum payment can help you reduce your credit card balance faster and save on interest charges.
2. Use Balance Transfer Cards - Balance transfer cards offer low or zero percent interest rates for a limited time, allowing you to transfer high-interest debt to a lower interest rate.
3. Create a Payment Plan - Creating a payment plan that prioritizes paying off high-interest debt first can help you pay off your credit card debt faster.
4. Avoid New Debt - Avoid using your credit card for new purchases while you are trying to pay off your balance.
5. Consider Debt Consolidation - Debt consolidation can combine all your debts into a single payment, making it easier to manage your debt.

Managing Student Loan Debt:

1. Understand Your Repayment Plan Options - Federal student loans offer several repayment plan options, including income-driven repayment plans, which adjust your monthly payment based on your income and family size.
2. Make Payments on Time - Late payments can damage your credit score and lead to additional fees and penalties.

3. Consider Consolidation or Refinancing - Consolidating or refinancing your student loans can help you lower your interest rate and simplify your payments.
4. Explore Loan Forgiveness Programs - There are various loan forgiveness programs available to borrowers who work in certain fields, such as public service or education.
5. Communicate with Your Lender - If you are struggling to make payments, communicate with your lender as soon as possible. They may be able to offer you forbearance or deferment options.

Understanding Credit Scores:

1. Payment History - Payment history is the most critical factor in determining your credit score. Late payments, missed payments, and delinquencies can negatively impact your score.
2. Credit Utilization - Credit utilization is the amount of credit you are currently using compared to your credit limits. High credit utilization can negatively impact your score.
3. Length of Credit History - The length of your credit history can positively impact your score. The longer you have a credit account in good standing, the better.
4. Types of Credit - Having a mix of credit types, such as installment loans and credit cards, can positively impact your score.
5. New Credit - Opening new credit accounts can negatively impact your score, particularly if you open several accounts at once.

In conclusion, understanding the different types of credit, managing credit card and student loan debt, and understanding credit scores are crucial elements of credit and debt management. By implementing these strategies, you can improve your credit score, reduce your debt, and achieve financial stability.

Debt can be a double-edged sword when it comes to personal finance. While it can cause financial stress and negatively impact credit scores, it can also be used as a tool for financial freedom. Here are five ways to use debt as a tool for financial freedom:

1. Invest in Yourself: One way to use debt as a tool for financial freedom is to invest in yourself. This could include taking out student loans to pursue higher education, or taking out a business loan to start a business. For example, if you want to start your own business, taking out a loan to invest in inventory or marketing can help get your business off the ground. Once the business becomes profitable, you can use the profits to pay off the debt.

2. Consolidate Debt: Consolidating debt is another way to use debt as a tool for financial freedom. By consolidating high-interest debt into a single loan with a lower interest rate, you can save money on interest charges and pay off your debt faster. For example, if you have multiple credit card debts with high interest rates, you could consolidate them into a personal loan with a lower interest rate.

3. Invest in Real Estate: Real estate can be a great way to build wealth and generate passive income. One way to invest in real estate is to take out a mortgage to purchase a rental property. The rental income can be used to pay off the

mortgage and generate passive income. For example, if you purchase a rental property for $200,000 with a mortgage and rent it out for $1,500 per month, the rental income can be used to pay off the mortgage and generate additional income.

4. Build Credit: Building credit is important for financial stability and can be used as a tool for financial freedom. By using credit responsibly and making payments on time, you can build a strong credit history and improve your credit score. This can help you qualify for lower interest rates on loans and credit cards, which can save you money in the long run.

5. Leverage Low-Interest Debt: Finally, using low-interest debt to invest in high-return investments can be a way to use debt as a tool for financial freedom. For example, taking out a low-interest rate loan to invest in the stock market or real estate can generate a higher return on investment than the interest paid on the loan. However, this strategy requires careful research and risk management.

It's important to note that using debt as a tool for financial freedom requires careful planning and management. It's important to only take on debt that can be managed and paid off responsibly, and to avoid high-interest debt that can cause financial stress. It's also important to have a clear plan for paying off debt and using it to achieve financial goals.

Using debt to save taxes is a common strategy used by many wealthy individuals. Here are some techniques that millionaires use to leverage debt for tax savings:

1. Use mortgage interest deductions: Homeowners can deduct mortgage interest paid on their primary residence and a second home, up to a combined limit of $750,000 in mortgage debt. By taking advantage of this tax deduction, homeowners can reduce their taxable income and save money on their taxes.

Example: John owns a home with a $500,000 mortgage. He pays $15,000 in mortgage interest in a year. By deducting the mortgage interest from his taxable income, John can save money on his taxes.

2. Use business debt deductions: Business owners can deduct interest paid on business loans and credit lines. By taking advantage of this tax deduction, business owners can reduce their taxable income and save money on their taxes.

Example: Sarah owns a small business and has a $50,000 business loan. She pays $5,000 in interest on the loan in a year. By deducting the interest from her taxable income, Sarah can save money on her taxes.

3. Use student loan interest deductions: Individuals can deduct up to $2,500 in student loan interest paid each year. By taking advantage of this tax deduction, individuals can reduce their taxable income and save money on their taxes.

Example: Mark has $30,000 in student loan debt and pays $1,500 in interest on the loans in a year. By deducting the student loan interest from his taxable income, Mark can save money on his taxes.

4. Use investment interest deductions: Individuals can deduct investment interest paid on loans used to purchase investments such as stocks, bonds, and mutual funds. By taking advantage of this tax deduction, individuals can reduce their taxable income and save money on their taxes.

Example: Jane has $100,000 invested in stocks and takes out a $20,000 margin loan to purchase more stocks. She pays $1,000 in interest on the margin loan in a year. By deducting the investment interest from her taxable income, Jane can save money on her taxes.

5. Use home equity loans: Homeowners can use home equity loans to pay off high-interest debt, such as credit card debt. The interest paid on home equity loans is tax-deductible up to $100,000.

Example: Tom has $20,000 in credit card debt with an interest rate of 18%. He takes out a $20,000 home equity loan with an interest rate of 6% to pay off the credit card debt. By using the home equity loan, Tom can save money on interest payments and deduct the interest paid on his taxes.

6. Use margin loans: Investors can use margin loans to purchase more stocks and investments. The interest paid on margin loans is tax-deductible.

Example: Lisa has $50,000 in stocks and takes out a $10,000 margin loan to purchase more stocks. She pays $500 in interest on the margin loan in a year. By deducting the investment interest from her taxable income, Lisa can save money on her taxes.

7. Use personal loans for investments: Individuals can use personal loans to invest in stocks, bonds, and mutual funds. The interest paid on personal loans used for investment purposes is tax-deductible.

Example: Mike takes out a $10,000 personal loan to invest in stocks. He pays $500 in interest on the loan in a year. By deducting the investment interest from his taxable income, Mike can save money on his taxes.

8. Use car loans for business purposes: Business owners can deduct interest paid on car loans used for business purposes. By taking advantage of this tax deduction, business owners can use car loans to save money on taxes while financing their business vehicles. For example, a small business owner who needs a delivery van can purchase the vehicle with a car loan and deduct the interest on the loan as a business expense on their tax return. This reduces the

amount of taxable income for the business, resulting in lower taxes owed.

9. Refinance high-interest debt: Another way to use debt as a tool for financial freedom is to refinance high-interest debt. For example, if an individual has credit card debt with a high interest rate, they may be able to obtain a personal loan at a lower interest rate and use it to pay off the credit card debt. This can result in lower monthly payments and savings on interest charges.

10. Leverage debt for investments: Some wealthy individuals and businesses use debt to leverage their investments. For example, an investor may use a margin account to purchase stocks, borrowing funds from the brokerage firm at a low interest rate. If the stocks increase in value, the investor can earn a higher return on their investment, even after paying the interest on the loan.

11. Use debt to purchase income-generating assets: Debt can also be used to purchase income-generating assets, such as rental properties or dividend-paying stocks. By using debt to purchase these assets, individuals and businesses can generate income that exceeds the cost of borrowing. This can result in long-term financial gain and greater financial stability.

12. Take advantage of tax-advantaged debt: Finally, some types of debt offer tax advantages that can help individuals and businesses save money. For example, a mortgage on a primary residence allows homeowners to deduct the interest paid on their mortgage on their tax return, resulting in lower taxes owed.

Similarly, student loan interest is tax deductible up to a certain amount, making it a tax-advantaged form of debt.

In summary, debt can be used as a tool for financial freedom if used wisely and strategically. By taking advantage of tax deductions, refinancing high-interest debt, leveraging debt for investments, using debt to purchase income-generating assets, and utilizing tax-advantaged debt, individuals and businesses can save money, build wealth, and achieve greater financial stability. However, it's important to remember that taking on too much debt can lead to financial hardship and should be approached with caution.

"A bank is a place where they lend you an umbrella in fair weather and ask for it back when it begins to rain." - Robert Frost

Chapter 5: Retirement Planning

"Retirement is not a time to retire from your life, but a time to begin a new life with new opportunities." - Catherine Pulsifer

Retirement is a time when people want to relax and enjoy life without worrying about finances. To achieve that, planning for retirement is critical. This chapter covers everything from retirement savings plans to retirement income sources, to help readers develop a comprehensive retirement plan.

Retirement Savings Plans

1. 401(k) Plans: A 401(k) is a retirement plan sponsored by an employer that allows employees to save for retirement through automatic payroll deductions. Contributions to a 401(k) are tax-deferred, meaning that taxes on the contributions and earnings are not paid until withdrawals are made during retirement.
2. Individual Retirement Accounts (IRAs): IRAs are personal retirement accounts that allow individuals to contribute to their retirement savings. Contributions to a traditional IRA may be tax-deductible, and earnings grow tax-deferred. Roth IRAs are funded with after-tax dollars, but withdrawals in retirement are tax-free.
3. Simplified Employee Pension (SEP) Plan: A SEP plan is a retirement plan for self-employed individuals or small business owners. It allows for higher contribution limits than traditional or Roth IRAs, and contributions are tax-deductible.
4. Solo 401(k) Plans: A Solo 401(k) plan is similar to a traditional 401(k) plan, but it is designed for self-employed individuals. It allows for higher contribution limits and tax-deferred growth of investments.
5. Defined Benefit Plans: Defined benefit plans are employer-sponsored retirement plans that guarantee a specific retirement benefit to employees. The employer bears the investment risk and is responsible for funding the plan.

Types of Retirement Accounts

1. Traditional IRA: A traditional IRA allows for tax-deductible contributions and tax-deferred earnings until withdrawal.

2. Roth IRA: A Roth IRA is funded with after-tax dollars, but withdrawals in retirement are tax-free.
3. 401(k): A 401(k) plan allows for tax-deferred contributions and tax-deferred growth of investments until withdrawal.
4. 403(b): A 403(b) is a retirement plan for employees of non-profit organizations, schools, and government agencies. It allows for tax-deferred contributions and tax-deferred growth of investments until withdrawal.
5. SEP IRA: A SEP IRA is a retirement plan for self-employed individuals or small business owners. It allows for tax-deductible contributions and tax-deferred earnings until withdrawal.
6. **Retirement Planning Strategies**
1. Start Saving Early: The earlier an individual starts saving for retirement, the more time their investments have to grow. Starting early also means that smaller contributions over a longer period can accumulate into a substantial retirement fund.
2. Diversify Investments: Investing in a variety of assets, such as stocks, bonds, and mutual funds, can help spread out risk and maximize returns.
3. Monitor and Adjust Investments: As people get closer to retirement, it's important to adjust investment portfolios to reflect lower risk tolerance.
4. Consider a Financial Advisor: A financial advisor can help develop a comprehensive retirement plan and manage investments.
5. Plan for Healthcare Costs: Healthcare costs are likely to increase during retirement. Planning for these expenses can help ensure that they don't derail a retirement plan.

Retirement Income Sources

1. Social Security: Social Security is a government-run retirement benefit program that provides retirement, disability, and survivor benefits to eligible individuals.
2. Pension Plans: Pension plans are employer-sponsored retirement plans that provide a guaranteed income stream in retirement.
3. Retirement Savings Accounts: Retirement savings accounts, such as IRAs and 401(k) plans, provide a source of income in retirement.
4. Annuities: An annuity is an insurance product that pays out a fixed income stream in retirement.

5. Part-time work is another option for generating retirement income. Many retirees choose to work part-time to supplement their retirement savings and to stay active in the workforce. This can also help retirees delay the need to draw on their retirement accounts, allowing their savings to continue to grow. There are many part-time work opportunities available for retirees, such as working as a consultant, tutor, or customer service representative. Some retirees also choose to start their own business or pursue a hobby that can generate income, such as freelance writing or selling handmade crafts.

   For example, a retired accountant may choose to work part-time as a tax consultant during the tax season, providing valuable expertise and earning additional income. Alternatively, a retired teacher may choose to tutor students in their area of expertise or start a small business selling educational materials online.

It's important to note that while part-time work can provide additional income, it may also affect Social Security benefits if retirees start taking benefits before reaching full retirement age. Additionally, retirees should consider the physical demands of any part-time work they choose to undertake and ensure it does not negatively impact their health and well-being.

6. Required Minimum Distributions (RMDs):
Once an individual reaches age 72, they must begin taking RMDs from their tax-deferred retirement accounts, such as traditional IRAs, 401(k)s, and 403(b)s. The amount of the RMD is based on the account balance and the individual's life expectancy. Failing to take RMDs can result in substantial penalties. To avoid this, individuals should ensure that they are aware of the RMD rules and take the required distributions on time.

Example: John has a traditional IRA with a balance of $500,000. He turned 72 in January 2022 and is required to take an RMD for the year. Based on the IRS life expectancy tables, his RMD is $18,518. He must withdraw this amount by December 31, 2022, to avoid penalties.

7. Retirement Income Sources:

Retirement income can come from a variety of sources, including Social Security benefits, pension plans, and personal savings. It is important to consider all potential sources of retirement income when creating a retirement plan.

Example: Mary is retiring at age 65 and will have a monthly Social Security benefit of $1,500. She also has a pension plan that will provide her with $2,000 per month. In addition, she has personal savings of $500,000 that she plans to draw down over the course of her retirement.

8. Long-Term Care:

As individuals age, the likelihood of needing long-term care increases. Long-term care can be expensive and can quickly deplete retirement savings. To mitigate this risk, individuals can purchase long-term care insurance, which can cover the costs of nursing home care, assisted living, and in-home care.

Example: Tom is 60 years old and is concerned about the potential costs of long-term care. He decides to purchase a long-term care insurance policy that will pay up to $300 per day for up to five years of care. The policy has a premium of $4,000 per year.

9. Catch-Up Contributions:

Individuals who are 50 or older can make additional contributions to their retirement accounts, known as catch-up contributions. These contributions allow individuals to save more money for retirement and can help make up for any previous years where they were unable to save as much.

Example: Susan is 55 years old and has a 401(k) plan through her employer. She is eligible to make catch-up contributions of up to $6,500 per year in addition to the regular contribution limit of $19,500. Susan decides to take advantage of the catch-up contribution option and contributes the maximum allowed.

10.   Roth Conversions:

Individuals with traditional IRAs or 401(k)s can convert their accounts to Roth accounts, which offer tax-free withdrawals in retirement. While there are taxes due on the amount converted, the benefits of tax-free withdrawals can outweigh the costs.

Example: Mike has a traditional IRA with a balance of $250,000. He is in a lower tax bracket this year and decides to convert his traditional IRA to a Roth IRA.

He will owe taxes on the $250,000 at his current tax rate, but will not owe taxes on any withdrawals made in retirement.

"It's not how much money you make, but how much money you keep, how hard it works for you, and how many generations you keep it for." - Robert Kiyosaki

Chapter 6: Insurance and Risk Management

"Insurance is not about avoiding risks, it's about protecting yourself from the consequences of those risks."

Introduction:

Insurance and risk management are crucial aspects of financial planning. In this chapter, we will discuss various types of insurance, how to choose the right insurance coverage, risk management strategies, and how insurance fits into estate planning.

Types of Insurance:

1. Life Insurance - A policy that pays out a sum of money to the policyholder's beneficiaries upon the policyholder's death.
2. Health Insurance - A policy that covers medical expenses incurred by the policyholder or their dependents.
3. Disability Insurance - A policy that provides income replacement in case the policyholder becomes unable to work due to a disability.
4. Long-Term Care Insurance - A policy that covers expenses incurred for long-term care services in case the policyholder becomes unable to perform activities of daily living.
5. Property and Casualty Insurance - A policy that provides protection against property damage or loss and liability claims.

Choosing the Right Insurance Coverage:

1. Assess Your Needs - Determine the type and amount of insurance coverage required based on your individual needs and circumstances.
2. Research Insurance Providers - Compare policies from different providers and evaluate their reputation, customer service, and financial stability.
3. Consider Deductibles and Premiums - Determine the deductible and premium amounts that fit your budget and coverage needs.
4. Review Policy Exclusions and Limitations - Carefully read the policy terms and conditions to understand any exclusions or limitations.
5. Evaluate Policy Benefits - Compare the benefits offered by different policies and choose the one that provides the most comprehensive coverage for your needs.

Risk Management Strategies:

1. Identify Risks - Determine potential risks and evaluate their likelihood and impact.
2. Reduce Risks - Take steps to mitigate identified risks, such as installing safety features, implementing policies and procedures, or obtaining insurance coverage.
3. Transfer Risks - Transfer risk through insurance coverage or contractual agreements.
4. Accept Risks - Accept some risks that cannot be avoided or transferred and take steps to minimize the impact in case they occur.

Insurance and Estate Planning:

1. Include Insurance in Estate Planning - Determine the type and amount of insurance required to meet estate planning objectives.
2. Name Beneficiaries - Designate beneficiaries for insurance policies to ensure they are distributed according to your wishes.
3. Update Policies Regularly - Review and update insurance policies regularly to ensure they align with changes in your circumstances and estate planning objectives.

Conclusion:

Insurance and risk management are essential components of financial planning. By choosing the right insurance coverage, implementing risk management strategies, and incorporating insurance into estate planning, individuals can protect their financial security and achieve long-term financial goals.

"The biggest risk is not taking any risk. In a world that's changing really quickly, the only strategy that is guaranteed to fail is not taking risks." - Mark Zuckerberg

Chapter 7: Tax Planning

"In this world, nothing can be said to be certain, except death and taxes." - Benjamin Franklin

Understanding the Tax System
- Tax brackets: Taxpayers should understand the federal income tax brackets and the tax rates that correspond to each bracket. By doing so, they can determine their taxable income and the tax liability they owe to the government.

- Taxable income: Taxable income is the income amount used to calculate an individual's or entity's income tax due. It is calculated by subtracting allowable deductions from the total income earned.
- Tax credits: Tax credits are direct reductions in the amount of tax owed, rather than deductions from taxable income. Taxpayers should understand the types of tax credits available to them, such as the child tax credit, earned income tax credit, and education tax credits.

Tax Planning Strategies

- Timing: Taxpayers can use timing strategies to shift income and deductions between tax years, in order to minimize their tax liability. This includes strategies such as accelerating or deferring income, and prepaying deductible expenses.
- Deductions: Taxpayers can maximize their deductions by itemizing their deductions rather than taking the standard deduction. This involves keeping track of all eligible expenses, such as mortgage interest, charitable donations, and medical expenses.
- Retirement accounts: Contributions made to retirement accounts, such as 401(k)s and IRAs, can reduce a taxpayer's taxable income and lower their tax liability.
- Tax-loss harvesting: This involves selling investments that have lost value in order to offset capital gains and reduce taxable income.
- Tax-efficient investments: Taxpayers can invest in tax-efficient investments, such as municipal bonds and index funds, in order to minimize the taxes they owe on investment gains.

Tax Deductions and Credits

- Charitable donations: Taxpayers can deduct charitable donations made to qualified organizations from their taxable income.
- Mortgage interest: Taxpayers can deduct the interest paid on their mortgage from their taxable income, up to a certain limit.
- Education expenses: Taxpayers can claim tax credits and deductions for education expenses, such as the American Opportunity Credit and the Lifetime Learning Credit.
- Medical expenses: Taxpayers can deduct medical expenses that exceed a certain percentage of their income.
- State and local taxes: Taxpayers can deduct state and local income, sales, and property taxes from their federal income tax.

Tax-Advantaged Investment Options

- 401(k) plans: Contributions to 401(k) plans are made with pre-tax dollars, which reduces taxable income and lowers tax liability.
- Traditional IRAs: Contributions made to traditional IRAs are also made with pre-tax dollars, and contributions may be tax-deductible.
- Roth IRAs: Contributions to Roth IRAs are made with after-tax dollars, but qualified distributions are tax-free.
- Health savings accounts (HSAs): Contributions made to HSAs are tax-deductible, and withdrawals used for qualified medical expenses are tax-free.
- 529 plans: Earnings from 529 plans used for qualified education expenses are tax-free, and some states offer tax deductions or credits for contributions made to 529 plans.

Example:

For example, a taxpayer in the 22% tax bracket who contributes $5,000 to their traditional IRA reduces their taxable income by $5,000. This results in a tax savings of $1,100. Alternatively, a taxpayer in the same tax bracket who contributes $5,000 to a Roth IRA does not reduce their taxable income, but qualified distributions in retirement will be tax-free.

Another example would be a taxpayer who makes a $2,000 donation to a qualified charitable organization. If their taxable income is $50,000, they could potentially reduce their tax liability by $440 (22% of $2,000) by deducting the donation from their taxable income.

Here are some examples of tax-advantaged investment options:

1. Individual Retirement Accounts (IRAs): Traditional and Roth IRAs are designed to help individuals save for retirement. Contributions to traditional IRAs are tax-deductible, while Roth IRA contributions are made with after-tax dollars. Earnings grow tax-free in both types of accounts, but withdrawals from traditional IRAs are taxed as income, while withdrawals from Roth IRAs are tax-free if certain conditions are met.

2. 401(k) Plans: 401(k) plans are employer-sponsored retirement plans that allow employees to contribute a portion of their income on a pre-tax basis. Employers may also match a portion of the employee's contributions. Earnings in the account grow tax-free until withdrawals are made.

3. Health Savings Accounts (HSAs): HSAs are tax-advantaged savings accounts that can be used to pay for qualified

medical expenses. Contributions to HSAs are tax-deductible, and earnings grow tax-free. Withdrawals used for qualified medical expenses are tax-free.

4. Municipal Bonds: Municipal bonds are issued by state and local governments to finance public projects. The interest earned on these bonds is exempt from federal income tax and may also be exempt from state and local taxes.

5. Real Estate Investments: Real estate investments can provide tax benefits such as depreciation deductions, mortgage interest deductions, and the ability to defer taxes on capital gains through 1031 exchanges.

Here are some tax planning strategies that individuals can use:

1. Maximize deductions: By taking advantage of available tax deductions, individuals can reduce their taxable income and lower their tax liability. Common deductions include mortgage interest, charitable contributions, and state and local taxes.

2. Contribute to tax-advantaged accounts: As mentioned above, contributions to tax-advantaged accounts such as IRAs and HSAs can lower an individual's taxable income and provide tax benefits.

3. Time income and deductions: By timing income and deductions appropriately, individuals can lower their overall tax liability. For example, they may choose to defer income until the following year or accelerate deductions into the current year.

4. Take advantage of tax credits: Tax credits provide a dollar-for-dollar reduction in an individual's tax liability. Examples of tax credits include the Earned Income Tax Credit and the Child Tax Credit.

5. Work with a tax professional: A tax professional can help individuals navigate the complex tax system and identify opportunities for tax savings. They can also ensure that individuals are complying with all tax laws and regulations.

In conclusion, tax planning is an important aspect of financial management that can help individuals and businesses reduce their tax liability and achieve their financial goals. By understanding the tax system, utilizing tax planning strategies, and taking advantage of tax-advantaged investment options, individuals can maximize their tax savings and improve their financial well-being.

"The hardest thing in the world to understand is the income tax." - Albert Einstein

Chapter 8: Estate Planning

"The greatest glory in living lies not in never falling, but in rising every time we fall." - Nelson Mandela

Estate planning is the process of arranging and distributing one's assets in a manner that minimizes taxes and maximizes the amount of the estate that is passed on to the heirs. It involves deciding how assets will be transferred, how taxes will be paid, and how medical decisions will be made in case of incapacity. Estate planning is important because it helps to ensure that the wealth that has been accumulated over a lifetime is distributed according to the wishes of the individual.

Importance of Estate Planning:

Estate planning is important for several reasons. Firstly, it helps to ensure that the assets of an individual are distributed according to their wishes. Secondly, it helps to reduce taxes that would be owed by the heirs. Thirdly, it helps to protect the assets from creditors and other potential liabilities. Lastly, it helps to ensure that medical decisions are made according to the wishes of the individual.

Types of Wills and Trusts:

Wills and trusts are two of the most common estate planning tools used to distribute assets. A will is a legal document that outlines the distribution of assets after an individual's death. It is important to have a will because it provides clear instructions on how assets should be distributed, who should be in charge of distributing the assets, and who should be the guardian of minor children.

Trusts, on the other hand, are legal entities that can hold assets and distribute them according to the wishes of the individual. Trusts can be used to reduce taxes, protect assets, and ensure that the assets are distributed according to the wishes of the individual.

There are several types of wills and trusts, including living trusts, testamentary trusts, revocable trusts, and irrevocable trusts. Living trusts are trusts that are created during the lifetime of the individual and can be changed or terminated at any time. Testamentary trusts, on the other hand, are created through a will and only become effective after the individual's death. Revocable trusts are trusts that can be changed or terminated at any time, while irrevocable trusts cannot be changed or terminated once they are created.

Choosing Executors and Trustees:

Executors and trustees are responsible for managing and distributing the assets of the estate. Executors are responsible for carrying out the instructions in the will and settling the debts of the estate. Trustees, on the other hand, are responsible for managing the assets that have been placed in a trust.

They are responsible for investing the assets, making distributions to beneficiaries, and ensuring that the terms of the trust are followed.

When choosing an executor or trustee, it is important to choose someone who is trustworthy, organized, and has a good understanding of the estate planning process. It is also important to choose someone who is willing to take on the responsibilities of being an executor or trustee.

Estate Planning for Business Owners:

Estate planning for business owners involves determining what will happen to the business after the owner's death. Business owners need to decide whether they want to transfer the business to their heirs, sell the business, or dissolve the business. They also need to decide how the business will be managed if the owner becomes incapacitated.

One common estate planning tool used by business owners is a buy-sell agreement. A buy-sell agreement is an agreement between the owners of a business that outlines what will happen to the business if one of the owners dies or becomes incapacitated. The agreement usually requires the surviving owners to buy the deceased or incapacitated owner's share of the business at a predetermined price.

In addition to buy-sell agreements, business owners can also use trusts to transfer their business assets to their heirs. Trusts can be used to reduce taxes, protect assets, and ensure that the business is transferred according to the wishes of the individual.

In conclusion, personal finance is a crucial aspect of our lives and requires careful planning and execution. The topics covered in this book, such as budgeting, credit and debt management, retirement planning, tax planning, and estate planning, are all essential components of a well-rounded personal finance plan. By following the guidelines and strategies provided in each chapter, individuals can make informed financial decisions and take control of their financial future. It is important to understand that financial planning is not a one-time task but rather a continuous process that requires ongoing evaluation and adjustment.

By creating a budget, managing debt, saving for retirement, taking advantage of tax deductions and credits, and planning for the distribution of assets after death, individuals can achieve financial freedom and security.
It is important to seek professional advice when necessary and to stay informed about changes in laws and regulations that may affect personal finances. With dedication and discipline, anyone can achieve their financial goals and enjoy a comfortable and secure future.

"The will to succeed is important, but what's more important is the will to prepare." - Bobby Knight

Chapter 9: Financial Tools for Business Owners.

"A business that makes nothing but money is a poor business." - Henry Ford

Financial Management for Small Business Owners:

Financial management is a critical aspect of any successful business. It involves managing a company's financial resources to ensure that they are being used efficiently and effectively. Small business owners need to have a solid understanding of financial management to make informed decisions about their business operations.

One way to manage finances is to create a budget. A budget outlines projected income and expenses, providing a roadmap for a company's finances. Small business owners can use budgeting software, such as QuickBooks or Xero, to track income and expenses, manage invoices, and generate financial reports. Another important tool for financial management is cash flow analysis. Cash flow analysis helps business owners understand their company's inflows and outflows of cash. By identifying any potential cash flow issues, small business owners can make informed decisions to address these problems before they become too severe.

Accounting Software:

Accounting software is a crucial tool for small business owners. It enables them to track income and expenses, create invoices, manage payrolls, and generate financial reports. QuickBooks, Xero, and FreshBooks are some popular accounting software options.

Using accounting software can help business owners save time and avoid errors that can lead to financial complications. For example, invoicing software can automate the process of generating and sending invoices to clients, reducing the chances of human error. Additionally, payroll software can streamline the process of paying employees, ensuring that all employees receive accurate paychecks on time.

Business Loans and Financing Options:

Small businesses often require additional capital to expand operations or cover expenses. Business loans and financing options are two ways to obtain funding.

Business loans typically come from banks or other financial institutions. They require collateral, such as property or equipment, to secure the loan. Business owners must have a good credit score and provide detailed financial information to obtain a loan.

Financing options, such as venture capital or angel investing, involve investors providing capital to a business in exchange for a stake in the company. This type of financing is often used by startup companies with high growth potential.

Business Insurance:

Business insurance is a crucial component of financial tools for business owners. It is a type of insurance that is specifically designed to protect businesses against financial losses resulting from unforeseen events.

The following are some common types of business insurance:
1. General liability insurance: This type of insurance is designed to cover the costs associated with third-party bodily injury or property damage claims. For example, if a customer slips and falls in your store and files a lawsuit against your business, general liability insurance can help cover the legal costs and any settlement or judgment that may result from the lawsuit.
2. Property insurance: This type of insurance covers damage or loss to a business's physical assets, such as buildings, inventory, and equipment, due to events such as fire, theft, or natural disasters. For example, if a fire damages your business property and destroys your inventory, property insurance can help cover the costs of repairing or replacing your property and inventory.
3. Workers' compensation insurance: This type of insurance is designed to cover the costs associated with workplace injuries and illnesses. For example, if an employee is injured on the job and needs medical treatment and time off work, workers' compensation insurance can help cover the costs of medical treatment and lost wages.
4. Professional liability insurance: This type of insurance, also known as errors and omissions insurance, is designed to

cover the costs associated with professional mistakes or negligence. For example, if a client sues your business for giving them bad advice or making a mistake that causes them financial harm, professional liability insurance can help cover the costs of defending against the lawsuit and any settlement or judgment that may result.

5. Cyber liability insurance: This type of insurance is designed to cover the costs associated with data breaches and other cyber incidents. For example, if your business experiences a data breach and customer data is compromised, cyber liability insurance can help cover the costs of notifying affected customers, providing credit monitoring services, and defending against any lawsuits that may result.

It is important for business owners to carefully assess their insurance needs and work with an experienced insurance broker to determine the right types and levels of coverage for their business. By having the right insurance coverage in place, business owners can protect themselves against financial losses resulting from unexpected events and ensure the long-term success of their business.

Chapter 10: Financial Planning for Life Events

"When written in Chinese, the word 'crisis' is composed of two characters. One represents danger and the other represents opportunity." - John F. Kennedy

Life is full of unexpected events that can have a significant impact on our finances. In Chapter 10, we will discuss financial planning for various life events such as marriage, divorce, career changes, and health issues.

Planning for Marriage and Family:

Financial planning is a crucial aspect of preparing for marriage and building a family. It requires careful consideration and planning to ensure that you and your family are financially stable and prepared for any challenges that may arise. Some of the important aspects of financial planning for marriage and family include setting financial goals, creating a budget, building an emergency fund, planning for major life events (such as buying a home or having a child), and establishing a plan for long-term financial security.

For example, when setting financial goals, a couple may decide that they want to save for a down payment on a house or pay off student loans before starting a family. Creating a budget can help them manage their expenses and ensure that they are living within their means. Building an emergency fund can provide a safety net for unexpected expenses or income loss. Planning for major life events can involve researching and understanding the costs associated with each event and developing a plan to save or allocate funds accordingly. Establishing a plan for long-term financial security may involve investing in retirement accounts or considering life insurance policies.

Financial Planning for Divorce:

Divorce can have a significant impact on an individual's finances, and it is important to approach the process with a solid financial plan. Some of the key considerations when planning for divorce include determining the value of assets and debts, establishing a realistic budget, negotiating support payments (such as spousal or child support), and updating estate planning documents.

For example, when determining the value of assets and debts, it may be necessary to obtain appraisals or consult with financial experts. Establishing a realistic budget can involve analyzing current expenses and determining which expenses will need to be adjusted after the divorce. Negotiating support payments can be a complex process, requiring an understanding of state laws and guidelines. Updating estate planning documents, such as wills and beneficiary designations, is important to ensure that assets are distributed according to the individual's wishes.

Financial Planning for Career Changes:
Career changes can be both exciting and daunting, and they often involve financial considerations. Some of the important aspects of financial planning for career changes include assessing financial stability, developing a plan for income replacement, evaluating employee benefits, and considering additional education or training.

For example, when assessing financial stability, it may be necessary to determine how long savings or unemployment benefits can sustain the individual during the job search. Developing a plan for income replacement may involve considering part-time work or freelance opportunities while searching for a new job. Evaluating employee benefits can be important, as some benefits may be lost or changed during a career change. Considering additional education or training may be necessary to qualify for certain positions or industries.

Financial Planning for Health Issues:

Health issues can have a significant impact on an individual's finances, and it is important to develop a plan to manage the associated costs. Some of the important aspects of financial planning for health issues include understanding insurance coverage, creating a budget for medical expenses, exploring financial assistance options, and establishing a plan for long-term care.

For example, understanding insurance coverage may involve researching the terms and limitations of insurance policies or consulting with a healthcare provider. Creating a budget for medical expenses can help an individual manage their finances and plan for future costs.

Exploring financial assistance options, such as Medicaid or charitable organizations, can provide additional support for medical expenses. Establishing a plan for long-term care may involve researching and selecting a long-term care facility or considering long-term care insurance policies.

In conclusion, financial planning for life events is an essential part of overall financial planning. Life events such as marriage, divorce, career changes, and health issues can significantly impact one's finances. It is crucial to plan and prepare for these events in advance to minimize their financial impact.

Planning for marriage and family involves setting financial goals, establishing a budget, and creating a plan for savings and investments. Proper planning can help couples achieve their financial goals and create a stable financial future for their family.

Financial planning for divorce involves understanding the financial implications of the divorce, including the division of assets and liabilities. It is essential to work with a financial planner to ensure that one's financial future is secure after the divorce.

Career changes can be exciting, but they can also bring about significant financial changes. Proper financial planning can help individuals navigate these changes and ensure a smooth transition.
Health issues can have a significant financial impact on individuals and families. Financial planning for health issues involves preparing for the unexpected costs of healthcare and creating a plan to cover these expenses.

Overall, financial planning for life events is an ongoing process that requires careful consideration and planning. By being proactive and seeking professional advice when necessary, individuals can navigate life's events with financial stability and security.

Taking action to achieve financial stability is the most crucial step. It requires discipline, commitment, and consistent effort. Some key elements and rules to keep in mind when taking action to achieve financial stability include:

1. Setting Financial Goals: Clearly define your short-term and long-term financial goals. Make sure they are specific, measurable, achievable, realistic, and time-bound (SMART).

Example: Short-term financial goal - Paying off credit card debt within six months by making extra payments each month.

2. Creating a Budget: Develop a budget that aligns with your financial goals and helps you manage your income and expenses effectively.

Example: Create a monthly budget that allocates a certain percentage of your income to savings, investments, and debt payments, while covering essential living expenses.

3. Managing Debt: Develop a plan to manage and reduce debt effectively, including credit card debt, student loans, and other outstanding debts.

Example: Make a plan to pay off higher interest debts first and allocate extra funds towards debt payments while avoiding taking on unnecessary debt.

4. Saving and Investing Wisely: Develop a savings and investment strategy that aligns with your financial goals and risk tolerance. Diversify your investment portfolio to spread risk and maximize returns.

Example: Invest in a mix of stocks, bonds, and other investment options based on your risk tolerance and long-term financial goals.

5. Retirement Planning: Plan for your retirement by contributing to retirement accounts, such as 401(k)s or IRAs, and understanding different retirement income sources, such as Social Security and pensions.

Example: Maximize your contributions to retirement accounts and explore different retirement income sources to ensure a comfortable retirement.

6. Tax Planning: Understand the tax system and implement tax planning strategies to minimize your tax liabilities and take advantage of tax-advantaged investment options.

Example: Utilize tax-advantaged investment options, such as a Health Savings Account (HSA) or a 529 college savings plan, to save on taxes.

7. Estate Planning: Develop an estate plan that includes wills, trusts, and other legal documents to protect your assets and ensure your wishes are carried out after your death.

Example: Consult with an estate planning attorney to create a comprehensive estate plan that aligns with your financial goals and family's needs.

8. Risk Management and Insurance: Identify and manage potential risks by having appropriate insurance coverage, such as health insurance, life insurance, disability insurance, and property insurance.

Example: Assess your insurance needs and ensure you have adequate coverage to protect against potential risks, such as illness, disability, or property damage.

9. Financial Tools for Business Owners: If you are a business owner, implement effective financial management strategies, utilize accounting software, explore financing options, and protect your business with appropriate insurance coverage.

"It is not in the pursuit of happiness that we find fulfillment, it is in the happiness of pursuit." - Denis Waitley

Chapter 11: Conclusion

"The future belongs to those who believe in the beauty of their dreams." - Eleanor Roosevelt

Financial stability brings many benefits, including peace of mind, security, and the ability to achieve one's goals. When you have financial stability, you can be confident that you are prepared for any unexpected expenses, emergencies, or life events that may arise.

This level of preparedness allows you to focus on your personal and professional goals without worrying about the financial impact of these events.

To achieve long-term financial stability, you need to take a strategic approach to your finances. This includes setting financial goals and creating a plan to achieve them. The plan should be realistic and tailored to your individual circumstances, taking into account factors such as your income, expenses, debt, and savings.

One effective technique for achieving long-term financial stability is to create a budget. A budget allows you to track your income and expenses and identify areas where you can save money. By setting a realistic budget and sticking to it, you can reduce your expenses, pay off debt, and increase your savings.

Another essential aspect of long-term financial planning is investing. Investing your money allows it to grow over time, helping you achieve your financial goals. There are many different types of investments, including stocks, bonds, mutual funds, and real estate. Each type of investment has its own risks and benefits, and it's important to understand these before investing your money.

Planning for retirement is also a crucial part of long-term financial planning. Retirement planning involves setting aside money for your future retirement expenses, such as housing, healthcare, and living expenses. Retirement planning can include contributing to a 401(k) or IRA, and making sure you have a diversified investment portfolio to reduce risk.

Achieving financial stability requires action, and the book provides practical steps to take to achieve this goal. These steps include setting financial goals, creating a budget, reducing debt, increasing savings, and investing wisely. The book also emphasizes the importance of seeking professional financial advice to ensure that you are making the best decisions for your individual circumstances.

In conclusion, achieving financial stability and long-term financial planning are essential for achieving personal and professional goals, reducing stress, and living a fulfilling life. The techniques and strategies discussed in the book provide a roadmap for achieving financial stability and long-term financial success. By following these steps and seeking professional advice, you can take control of your finances and achieve your financial goals.

"Financial freedom is available to those who learn about it and work for it." - Robert Kiyosaki

INDEX

Budgeting: The process of creating a plan for how to spend and save money. Budgeting can help individuals and businesses manage their finances, prioritize expenses, and reach financial goals.

Business Insurance: Insurance policies designed to protect businesses from financial losses due to accidents, property damage, liability claims, and other risks. Business insurance can include general liability insurance, professional liability insurance, property insurance, and workers' compensation insurance, among others.

Business Loans: Loans provided to businesses by banks, credit unions, or other financial institutions. Business loans may be used for a variety of purposes, such as starting a new business, expanding an existing business, or financing equipment or inventory.

Credit Scores: A numerical rating assigned to individuals that reflects their creditworthiness. Credit scores are used by lenders to assess the risk of lending money to individuals and can impact the terms of loans, including interest rates and repayment periods.

Diversification: The process of spreading investments across different types of assets, such as stocks, bonds, and cash, to manage risk. Diversification can help protect against losses in any one asset class and potentially improve overall investment returns.

Estate Planning: The process of creating a plan for how an individual's assets will be managed and distributed after their death. Estate planning may involve the creation of a will, trust, or other legal documents to ensure that assets are distributed according to the individual's wishes.

Financial Planning: The process of creating a plan for how to manage and invest money in order to meet financial goals. Financial planning may involve budgeting, saving, investing, and managing debt, among other strategies.

Health Savings Accounts: A type of savings account that allows individuals to save money tax-free to pay for qualified medical expenses. HSAs may be offered as part of a high-deductible health insurance plan.

Insurance: A financial product that provides protection against financial losses due to accidents, property damage, liability claims, and other risks. Insurance policies may cover individuals, businesses, or property.

Investing: The process of using money to purchase assets with the expectation of generating a return on investment. Investing may involve purchasing stocks, bonds, mutual funds, or other types of assets.

Life Insurance: Insurance that pays out a sum of money upon the death of the insured individual. Life insurance can help provide financial support for loved ones after an individual's death.

Long-Term Care Insurance: Insurance that covers the costs of long-term care, such as nursing home care, for individuals who are unable to care for themselves due to illness or disability.

Mutual Funds: Mutual funds are investment vehicles that pool money from many investors to purchase a portfolio of stocks, bonds, or other securities. Mutual funds are managed by professional fund managers, who use the pooled money to invest in a diversified portfolio of assets. Investors in a mutual fund own a share of the fund and are entitled to a portion of the fund's earnings and assets.

Retirement Planning: Retirement planning is the process of setting financial goals and developing strategies to help you achieve those goals in your retirement years. Retirement planning involves estimating your retirement expenses, determining your sources of retirement income, and developing a plan to help you save and invest to meet your retirement goals.

Risk Management: Risk management is the process of identifying, assessing, and mitigating risks to an organization or individual. Risk management involves identifying potential risks, analyzing the likelihood and potential impact of those risks, and developing strategies to mitigate or avoid those risks.

Small Business: Small business refers to a business that is independently owned and operated, typically with fewer than 500 employees. Small businesses play a significant role in the economy, accounting for a large percentage of jobs and contributing to innovation and growth.

Social Security: Social Security is a government-run program that provides retirement, disability, and survivor benefits to eligible individuals. Social Security is funded through payroll taxes paid by workers and their employers, and benefits are paid out to eligible individuals based on their earnings history.

Stocks and Bonds: Stocks and bonds are two common types of investments. Stocks represent ownership in a company and are generally considered riskier but have the potential for higher returns. Bonds represent a loan to a company or government and are generally considered less risky but have lower potential returns.

Tax Planning: Tax planning is the process of managing your finances in a way that minimizes your tax liability. Tax planning involves evaluating your income, deductions, and credits to determine the best strategies for reducing your tax bill.

Trusts: A trust is a legal entity that holds assets on behalf of a beneficiary. Trusts are often used for estate planning purposes, as they can help manage assets and provide for the distribution of assets after death.

Wills: A will is a legal document that outlines how a person's assets should be distributed after their death. Wills can also be used to appoint guardians for minor children and name an executor to manage the estate. A will is an important part of estate planning, as it helps ensure that your assets are distributed according to your wishes.